T0208683

VLADIE:
STORY OF A TRAINER'S DOG

Maryann Keck

iUniverse, Inc.
Bloomington

Vladie: Story of a Trainer's Dog

iUniverse books may be ordered through booksellers or by contacting:

iUniverse
1663 Liberty Drive
Bloomington, IN 47403
www.iuniverse.com
1-800-Authors (1-800-288-4677)

ISBN: 978-1-4502-9875-9 (pbk)
ISBN: 978-1-4502-9876-6 (ebk)

Printed in the United States of America

iUniverse rev. date: 3/15/11

Prologue

I think it must have been around my twenty-fifth birthday and I felt so deflated, like I had wasted my life. I was overweight, had no boyfriend, no job or motivation and had no idea what to do with my life. My only reoccurring thought was in twenty-five more years, I will be fifty and what have I accomplished? What do I have to show for my existence on this earth? Answer- nothing.

In my more rational moments, I could list a few so-called achievements ranging from doing dance and piano recitals when I was a kid, to being a high school honor student and graduate. Then going to college to be an artist and selling some of my work to private parties as well as being featured in the college art/literary magazine and art shows. I could list my many hobbies over the years but I did not consider them to be worthy of a lifetime achievement award nor do I see the need to list them here and now.

I think my parents were concerned about me at this time, more than usual. (I am an only child so excessive worrying seems to go with that territory.) One day, my mother sat me down and voiced her concerns. She was sensitive, caring but indicated that I had her worried. She said I needed to get out more, stop hiding in my room and although she was proud of my artistic talents, she could tell (through my paintings and sketches) that I was not truly happy. At the time, I did not think I was depressed- yes, sometimes but not to the extent that I needed an intervention. My mother proceeded to tell me to start doing something I enjoyed like take up tennis-playing again or join a gym, do volunteer work somewhere but get out of my room more. Though I did not get angry, I did feel shame and hurt but it did motivate me to try. So that same afternoon, I called the gym in town and got some membership information. Since I have had animals all my life- (hamsters, dogs, chickens, rabbits and fish), I decided to call the local humane society that I remembered seeing in the local pet store doing adoptions. I got information about volunteering with them. So...this is where my story really begins.

Chapter One

My last dog, a cocker spaniel mix named Cuddles, had died from old age a few years prior and my mom was eager for me to get another dog but I adamantly refused. I was still missing Cuddles so I threw myself into the new plan to get out more.

I began volunteering for a local humane society, going to meetings and helping with the dog, cat adoptions at the pet store on weekends. It was not long before I was helping with fundraisers, getting donations and working two to three times a week. I was there as the humane society moved from one location to another, built a store, and hired a cruelty investigation officer. My parents helped too and we earned a reputation as great volunteers. This was also when I met my best friend, Renee who was also a volunteer.

I had seen many cute puppies during those years, volunteering but I was able to tend to their needs, help them get homes and say goodbye without too much sadness. It was not time for me to adopt. That was how I saw it and what I told myself.

Then one day, while at the pet store, volunteering, I was asked to work in the cat room, as I had done many times before. So while cleaning the cubicles, feeding and watering the cats, I saw a new arrival- a crème and golden-furred male cat. They had named him Julius and he was so cute. He just wanted attention and needed it. (He was a mess.) I had always liked cats but could not have one because I had been born with an allergy to all cats. So I cleaned him, tended to him for months until someone adopted him. For the first time I was very sad to see an animal in the humane society program get adopted. But that is a story for another time. The point being, my mom, seeing that I had really liked the cat thought perhaps I was finally getting ready to get another pet and began to encourage me to get a puppy. I knew she wanted me to be happy and that I loved dogs, but I was not sold. Even so, occasionally I found myself studying the dogs who were up for adoption alittle closer than I used to do. I had also chosen a name, if I were to ever get a dog- Vladie and yes, it's a vampire reference since I was into goth at the time.

As fate would have it, my parents and I went down to the humane society to help for a few hours and they had a travel carrier with five puppies in it. One of the staff had brought them in to be checked out and get their shots. Mom instantly picked two that she liked and said I should look at them. My dad pretended to ignore her, I think. (Don't get me wrong- he liked animals but whenever we tried to bring one into the house, he was usually less than thrilled.) Anyway, I was asked to clean the pups up since they had messed up the carrier in transit so I ended up playing with them- shepherd mix puppies; two girls, three boys, all siblings. The staff member, Jane explained that she had come to work two weeks before to find a cardboard box outside the door of the humane society with all the puppies in it- scared, crying and snuggled together with a note. All the note said was "the mother was hit by a car". The puppies were guessed to be about five weeks old. Jane had to bottle feed them every few hours for a couple of weeks and she kept them at her home until they were old enough to be spayed/ neutered and then put up for adoption. She also told us a bit about each one's personalities. One of the females, the darkest colored one, was the most calm. This pup was shy but she eventually came up to me after a short time of my sitting on the floor with them. Mom was sold. She said I should foster the pup so we could see if her older poodle, Baby would accept a new dog in the house. So I thought about it while I worked and I looked at that little face- the face that was mostly black with ears that could not stand up on their own yet and the tan markings above the ebony eyes that looked like eyebrows. By the end of my shift, I had made out the paperwork to be a humane society temporary foster parent. We bought a second-hand crate, (which is a handy training tool), some food and some toys and took the puppy home with us.

When we got home, I laid out an old vinyl shower curtain on the floor with some newspapers on it, built the crate, with help from my father and got the pup set up. I wanted to let her rest since she'd had a busy day and was still so young, I knew she would need a nap. So that is how I began to crate train her; it became her little safe den or sanctuary. She had towels for a bed and plastic food bowls. It was not long before her favorite past time was kicking the water bowl around. She quickly learned what a toy was and she preferred the big, stuffed ones. (One favorite was a large black and white zebra with gangly legs that squeaked.)

I fought down the urge to name her since I still was not positive that she was going to stay with me so I tried to keep calling her Blackie. That is what Jane had named her but I longed to call her the name I had chosen. Two weeks later, she was christened Vladie and she learned it fast. The day we had to take her back to the humane society to have her shots again, I feared they might not let me keep her. Having never fostered before, I did not know what to expect. After all, I was only a foster parent- anyone could show an interest in her either from her pictures in the newsletter or on the website and they could take her away. I tried to remind myself that she was not mine and that if they did have another family wanting to adopt her, I would have to let her go. I felt myself tense up as we entered the small building. This could be it, I thought. I held the handle of the carrier alittle tighter. I was met by the tall brunette staff worker, Mandy and she took the puppy after I got her out of the carrier. We took her in the back of the building and put her on the exam table. I watched closely- trying not to feel apprehension as Mandy got the shot needle out. Expertly, she gave Vladie the shot. The pup behaved herself; she did not cry or try to get away. I felt some relief when Mandy was done. She then informed me that the puppy needed to come back in a week to be taken to their vet to be spayed. Though I wanted it done and understood why it had to be done-(there are too many unwanted pets on this earth and the shelters are full), this idea scared me. (Surgeries of any kind- well anything medical fills me with dread, must be because of my childhood.) But since the humane society's policy stated that no cat or dog in their program could be adopted until they were spayed or neutered, I could only voice my concern and the desire to adopt Vladie afterward. (Oh, by the way, my mom's poodle was not so pleased to have a new little cousin but I trusted with training, Baby would come to accept Vladie, which she eventually did). So we took Vladie home again and I continued to work with her, play with her and felt myself growing more attached to her each day that passed.

I think it was during this time that I got really sick- a very bad cold. I had taken to sleeping in the room with Vladie but I was on the floor and she was usually in her crate. I was trying to train her that nighttime hours meant sleep and no play but I knew she was lonely so I spent the night in the room with her. But that's when I came down with the cold and I remember she wanted to play. She would romp over to me and try to pounce on my head or sometimes she would cuddle up and want to lay down but then shoot up and run around the room like some crazed winde-up toy. I felt bad that I could not respond as she wanted because I was so ill and I was afraid to handle her too much or breathe on her because I had been told that dogs can get colds from us, humans. So anytime I did handle her during my illness, I washed my hands first and kept my handling to a minimum. She did not seem to notice or care and once I began to feel better, I was able to give her more attention and cuddle time.

March 23, 2005, the day we brought Vladie back to the humane society to be spayed was hard on me. I was finally feeling better from the cold but was still alittle...off. I asked the staff member if I could put in the paperwork to adopt and she kindly explained I could not since it was against policy; Vladie had to be spayed first. So I had to wait. We wanted to drive her to the vet ourselves but again, the manager, Kelly said one of the staff had to do it. I am ashamed to say I got emotional at this point and had to walk away but Kelly saw. I understood Kelly's point but I was afraid for Vladie and did not like not being involved. Talk about being overly protective, right? I knew the staff member, Amy and I liked her a lot and I had her cell number so when she came and took Vladie, along with some other dogs, she said I could call her when they got out to the vet's office. I am sure that both Amy and Kelly thought my mom and I were too protective of the pup but I was feeling like she as already mine though I kept telling myself that she was not, not yet. So my mom and I started calling Amy after fourty-five minutes and she said that Vladie had gotten carsick but was okay. She said she would let the vet know that mom and I were going to pick Vladie up after her operation. Mom and I appreciated this. We knew that Amy would not be able to pick up all the pups until later that evening and we could not bear to think of Vladie stuck in a cubicle at the vet's, getting freaked out. We were there at the office after a long drive and when the vet technician brought little Vladie out, she was still groggy. I called her name and her little tail started to wag and she squirmed a bit. The vet tech said that was the most response Vladie had shown since Amy had brought her in. I smiled and took Vladie in my arms and started talking to her. Mom cooed over her and rubbed her head. We thanked the vet tech and took Vladie out to the car. She sat in my lap the entire time, getting a little squirmy at times. I had her borrowed carrier on the backseat in case but ended up not needing it.

It was a relief to get Vladie back home. I put her in her potty area to continue to potty train her. She was a good girl then I put her in her crate. Just so you know, in the beginning, her crate was not fancy as I have already described. Now, she had been upgraded to a nicer towel, a few toys and a chew bone were included. Since she was teething, I did not want to put anything fancy in with her yet because I knew I would come home to find only remnants of a plush bed or nice blanket left and my money would end up in the trash. She was happy with the new additions. I did however buy her a big stuffed doggie- this thing was five times her size and squishy. He was of a white and pale blue patchwork design and was just like a huge pillow for her. I put it in the crate for her to cuddle with so she would feel like her birth mother or littermates were there. She would lay next to it, rest her short legs, and small head on the toy's legs. I was sure to take a picture of that- how could I not? She would put herself to bed in the crate whenever she felt tired and I would find her asleep on her big doggie.

March 24th, 2005- the momentus day had arrived! Mom and I drove down to the humane society again to make out the adoption papers. I was still alittle nervous; not sure if they were going to let me adopt Vladie but Mandy was there and she walked me through the process. I remember her saying 'You don't need me to go all through this since you know it, right?" She was not being sarcastic or patronizing. She really did think that I was familiar with their adoption contract considering how long I had been volunteering with them at the adoption events. I had to point out that I had not been trained to be an adoption counselor; I was only the behind-the-scenes girl so Mandy laughed and went through the paperwork quick for me. I signed everything, agreeing to provide a safe and loving home, to bring Vladie back to be micro chipped and accept full responsibility for her medical care, food and grooming. I paid the eighty dollars adoption fee and Vladie was mine! I could have jumped for joy or done the irish jig but of course, I restrained myself. My mother was thrilled too and she happily chatted all the way home, congratulating me. I had to laugh at her excitement at the prospect of finally being a grandma. She surprised me when she said that she had been a little concerned that they might not have let us adopt Vladie after all. The process could have been worse. We got home and told my father that he was an official grandfather. He laughed and was very happy too.

When I got back home, I found Vladie safe, in the crate resting with her big puppy until she heard me. She stood up on her hinde legs, her little paws sticking through the wire of the crate, crying to be let out. I ignored her until she quieted down then I let her out. You might be thinking why did I wait? Well, if I had let her out while she was crying or barking, I would have reinforced the noise which is not what I wanted. I wanted her to learn to wait and be quiet then she gets the reward of what she wants. So I scooped her up, hugged her then put her down on her potty spot to do her business. She was more interested in playing but her bladder had other ideas. Then she was really ready to play. BRING ON THE TOYS!

As far as Vladie was concerned, a good toy was one that she could either yank the stuffing or squeaker out of, had tails, noses and ears that were meant to be chewed or plucked off. As I have previously stated, she had the large zebra toy with a long fuzz- ball tail and floppy ears. What do you think was the first things Mr. Zebra lost? You guessed right- (you get a biscuit), the tail and ears.

He was well loved. Another toy she enjoyed, besides the rubber balls and squeaky toys, was a rather large stuffed camel. That thing cost me fifteen bucks. Yeah, I know I lost my mind that day in the pet supply store but I knew she would love it so I paid the money. It lasted maybe a week or two. When I came into the room and found fuzzy snow all over the floor, I knew Mr. camel had gone to the big sahara playground in the sky. Vladie loved her toys. She even helped herself to Baby's now and then but she would share hers with Baby in return. I remember the big, bright pink, fuzzy dice she had that was connected by a fuzzy bungy rope. Vladie would drag it out into the living room and offer it to Baby and as soon as Baby would try to get her small mouth around the big dice, Vladie would start to pull it away. Baby, who never had a puppy to play with when she was young, did not know how to play with another dog so she had to learn, with Vladie's help. Vladie would growl alittle and go into playbow position, trying to entice Baby to grab the dice and pull. It took a few times but Baby eventually caught on and they began to play tug-of-war. Vladie was now Baby's size and Baby was years older than Vladie at this point. So, see you can teach an old dog new tricks!

But back to Vladie stealing Baby's toys. Mom still brings it up to me how Baby's blue and white stuffed panda bear had to be sewed up a few times after Vladie squashed the squeaker in it. Plus, how Baby's very first rubber toy-a mini pink piggy lost its tiny ears and nose, thanks to Vladie. My mother laughs about it but she STILL brings it up. Ahhh… the trials and tribulations of puppy hood.

Chapter Two

I think it was later in the week that I took Vladie into the busy pet store to see Mandy again, to get micro chipped. All dog and cat owners (in my opinion) should do this. (If your pet gets lost and is then found and taken to a shelter that has a microchip scanner, they can scan for the chip and find the identification number. Then the shelter calls the microchip company and they in turn call you so you know where to find your pet.) Cool, huh? So I carried Vladie into the catroom and believe me, that got all the cats' attention. Mandy got out the little needle. She pinched Vladie's skin near the back of the neck and between the shoulder blades-(which is the usual injection site for this) and literally, within two seconds, she said, "All done." Vladie had not felt a thing and I had the extra sense of security; knowing that if her collar and metal id tag, which all dogs and cats should wear also, were to get lost, there would be another chance of my getting her back. Mom and I then took Vladie back home and she needed a potty break though I have to admit she had already christened the petstore floor when we had first arrived there. Come to think of it, every time she went into that store, she always christened the floor... and it wasn't pretty. But anyway, once she got home she was ready for a short nap and lunch and then she was rarin' to go for playtime. She romped over to the toy pile and picked up one or two and then thrashed the toy around alittle. My father named this behavior- 'Bad Boy' and Vladie would roll around on the toy and toss it aside then go for another one. I began to teach her the toys' names and she was starting to distinguish one toy from the other with little difficulty. After she got tired of that, she would grab a toy in her little mouth and she would go as fast as her little legs would carry her down the hallway and out to the living room to find Baby.

Vladie liked Baby and wanted to play but Baby.... well, she was not so eager for a playmate. I remember one time Vladie hauled out the hot pink, large, fuzzy dice toy. Vladie took it out to Baby who just looked at the puppy as if she had lost her mind. Baby always had a wary kind of expression when Vladie would come out into her territory, so this time was no different. Baby growled and stared Vladie down- a classic signal from one dog to another. Baby was telling Vladie that she was in Baby's claimed area and she better follow the rules. (Dogs can help teach each other the rules of the house and establish their place in the household- it's called social learning). Vladie was still young, had not learned all her doggie language yet but she got that signal and dropped the toy then scampered under the wooden footstool in front of my mother's recliner. Of course, her running and hiding made Baby bark and charge. Baby backed off when Vladie got underneath the stool, her head resting on her small paws, just watching Baby. It was times like these that I started to see Vladie's personality starting to develop. She was going to be a submissive dog and that was good since Baby was an insecure/dominant one.

My mom was sitting in her chair and I was on the floor when I got Baby to back off and lay down. I then enticed Vladie out from under the stool with the toy. She would come, hesitantly but the prospect of a good game would override Baby's noisy warning. Vladie grabbed hold of the dice toy while I had the other end. She growled and pulled, tossing her head from side to side and sliding along over the rug as she tried to keep her footing. She would pull and growl some more and I would let her have the toy then she would scamper off and hurry back to me to start over again. Knowing what I know now, this was not the best game to teach Vladie and it's a controversial subject in the training world so in my opinion, don't do it. But if you are determined to then you have to teach the game to your dog in the correct way. The correct way is to remember some guidelines. First, YOU start the game and end the game. Second, do not pull- let the dog do it and no shaking the dog's head around. A pup's neck can get injured. Teach the dog to do 'Drop it' on command so when you are ready to claim the toy, the dog will let go of it. Claim the toy! This means that when you say 'Drop it' and the dog complies, then hug the toy or item to your chest, make eye contact with the dog and say, 'Mine'. This tells the dog that you are claiming the item. If it's a toy that the dog is permitted to have, then say 'Okay' as your release word and give the toy to the dog as you tell the dog to 'Take it'. Now, if it's an item that you don't want the dog to have, then claim the item as I have already stated, then give the dog a toy or item he can have and say "Take it'. This trade-off game helps get you out of tough situations. Anyways, I did however teach Vladie while playing this game, to give me the toy on command. We would play a bit then when I wanted her to let go, I would make eye contact and give the cue- 'Mine'. She learned to let go of the toy at this time and then after a few minutes, I would give the toy back to her and say, "Okay" then end the game. She learned, this way, not to be a resource guarder. What's that, you might ask? A dog who claims things like toys, food, etc and will not let go at all.)

So Vladie would then take the dice toy and drag the long tail around the floor. Baby started to show an interest. She approached, timidly but she seemed fascinated with this long toy that was bigger than she was. Baby then pawed it and Vladie shook the toy as best as she could without falling over from dizziness. Baby surprised all of us by grabbing the bungy cord part and daintily pulling it away. Vladie, seeing that Baby was trying to play, growled a little and went into playbow position. (You know that one- the front part of the body goes down while the butt is up in the air.) She was telling Baby to play but since Baby had not grown up in our house with another dog, she did not know this language so this was foreign to her. Still, the two dogs began to play tug much to my mother's and my enjoyment. We laughed as our doggies pulled and growled and slid around across the rug until Baby gave up. I would carry or call Vladie to come back down the hallway to our room for her potty break and her nap. She went into her crate slowly- she never did like to stop playing, but then she laid down with a thump next to her big doggie. She would give me a pathetic look before I turned away to turn on the cd player. I played Mozart and inspirational instrumentals for her to fall asleep to. She seemed to like it. Then I would go out of the room for awhile, smiling to myself and thinking what a great pup I had.

As I had said, Vladie's personality was starting to emerge more now as her body began to sprout up. Her ears were starting to stand up on their own more and her paws had grown but the rest of her still had to catch up. I could tell that she was still a shy dog, timid at times, especially around new things or in new environments. She was showing some signs of being very cautious and being slightly insecure. I did not want that insecurity to grow so when my mom mentioned dog training classes, I thought it was a good idea. Mom was concerned that Vladie was going to be a big, powerful dog and we had never had a powerful breed before so she feared we would not be able to handle her when Vladie grew up. I was not too concerned at that point but I did not want Vladie to grow up scared of everyone and everything.

So on one of our trips to the petstore, we signed up for the eight week dog training course. I had heard good things about one of the three trainers who taught there so I was not too worried. I remember the first day of class. Vladie had already gotten used to wearing the collar and walking on leash, though our actual loose leash walk still needed lots of help. My mom and I walked her into the training ring. Back then, the training area was next to the grooming department off to the side from the manager's office and the ring was a thick netting with poles that the trainers had to take down and put up every time they needed it. They had a trolley cart for their supplies. Toys were scattered on the floor and there were some folding chairs set up. I felt a little nervous, self-conscious when entering the ring. A young woman with a small dog was already there and another lady with a young son and their two rottweiler pups were just entering the ring as we were. These were Vladie's fellow students. The trainer was a middle-aged woman with blonde, wavy hair, tall and had a kind but commanding presence to her. Connie was her name and she was enthusiastic and knowledgable. She laid down the rules of the class, explained the course and then had us meet each other's dogs. She reached for Vladie, scooped her up and Vladie shocked all of us by screeching at the top of her voice which she had never done before. She had always been a quiet dog. I was so embarrassed especially when Connie's eyes widened and she said, "Oh noone's been coddling this pup, have they?" I could have melted down into the floor tiles at that moment. Connie proceeded to explain the necessity of proper socialization of our dogs. She then had us swap our puppies so that the pups got to meet and be petted by a stranger. I was nervous until Vladie was returned to me but I did NOT coddle her. She had to grow up to be a confident girl so I could not pamper or coo over her while she was in class. 'Course, Vladie's plan was to hide under my chair until the school bell rang. So much for socializing. I knew she and I had not started the class on the right paw.

By the end of the second week of class, Vladie was more relaxed in the training ring. I, on the other hand, was still nervous. The other small dog had quit the class but the two rotties were still there and those boys started to take an interest in Vladie. She was not too thrilled with their butt-sniffin' action but she eventually learned to try to play with them, occasionally. She would sneak in when they were not watching and steal a toy but when one or both of the rotties would catch her, the toy would be forgotten and the chase would be on. Vladie would high-tail it around the ring, until their owner or I distracted the boys with a better toy or treat.

It was also during this time that Vladie learned to LOVE treats. She never found a treat that she would not try at least once or twice. Connie would sit on the linoleum floor and try to teach a behavior to us, not always aware of Vladie sitting at her side, staring and waiting for the treat. Sometimes, Vladie actually snuck her snoot into the treat bag that Connie wore on her belt buckle. We would all laugh and I would try to get Vladie to leave Connie alone but Connie would laugh too for a second before she said, "Don't want to encourage pushy doggie behaviors." She would then proceed to redirect Vladie with a toy or to do a behavior. Back in those days, I was much more timid with people; afraid to do something stupid. So during classes I kind of hung back unless Connie instructed me to get out and work with Vladie in front of the other students. Then I would feel self-conscious and I now know I made Vladie skittish back then. As that well-known tv trainer says, dogs can sense our energy but at that time, I did not focus on spiritual, emotional connections to our dogs and Connie did not teach that. (She was a just-the-facts kind of gal). Still, we learned a lot through her lure and reward method and using positive reinforcement. Oh…and for those of you who might not be in the know on that subject; these are methods that many trainers use now by using praise, treats to help your dog learn commands. It also helps the dog make good associations with the world and their owners. To put it another way- you are at work, you do something your manager asks you to do, you do it well. You get a raise. There you go! Positive reinforcement.

So our lessons continued. Vladie had a bit of a hard time with a couple of the commands like 'Leave it' (leaving items alone that were within her reach), and the 'Come' or recall. The leash walk was also a challenge but it is for most dogs. Even so, Vladie was smart; she picked up on most of the commands and hand signals that Connie taught us, quickly. She was really good at 'Watch me' (making eye contact), and she was starting to communicate more. By that I mean she would cock her head and stare at my face, trying to figure out what I was saying to her. She was starting to look like she was laughing which became even more apparent as she got older. She always looked happy and in fact, my father would often call her "Happy Dog" or "Smiley".

When Vladie wasn't working, she was playing. I brought home a big ball from the store one day- one of the plastic balls that usually look like a marble/painted design of pastel colors, made for kids. Vladie was still small enough that the ball was just a little bit bigger than she was. She looked at it with a puzzled expression as I put it on the floor. I wanted to see if she would interact with it. She stepped up to it, staring intensely then she jumped back as it moved on it's own from a breeze coming into the room. She sniffed it and then walked around it, as if trying to sneak up on it from behind. Then she bumped it with her nose and I told her to get it. That did it! She kicked it with her paw and then kept bumping it around the room with her nose, getting more excited. She was so thrilled with her new toy! She liked to play soccer with it and it was so lightweight that it didn't hurt her face as she butted up against it or if it popped up at her. She had it bouncing up and down and off the wall and I thought for sure, something was going to get broken. That's why it's always good to puppy-proof your home, people, to avoid unnecessary breakage. If she got too jazzed, I told her to back off but if Vladie did not listen, the ball got taken away and put up on a shelf. This only happened once and she sat there for a second, waiting for it to fall back down to her. When it didn't and I turned my back, my little genius, pawed the plastic shelf and down the ball came right over her head. I can tell you, Vladie was very pleased with herself for that little manuever.

After a couple of days of playing indoor soccer with her new ball, I was out in the living room and Vladie had pushed the ball from her room out to me. Of course, Baby had an absolute barking fit when her sister came barreling in with this huge ball rolling around in front of her. (Remember, the ball was a lot bigger than Baby, as most things were.) So Baby's barking and charging at the ball, then running away while I was trying to clean the room. Vladie was totally oblivious to the chaos she had caused when I saw her reach over the top of the ball with her paw and kick it and I heard a….. psssssst sound. Vladie and I watched as the ball slowly deflated. I felt bad but was about to shrug it off until I saw Vladie's body language. Her head lowered as the ball got lower to the ground. Looking confused but when the ball was reduced to plastic pancake, I thought Vladie might cry, if dogs can cry. (I told ya she had an expressive face.) She really looked sad. She looked up at me as if I could do something and I wished I could have. She laid down next to her former playtoy and sulked for awhile. When she was not looking, I took it and threw it away, planning on replacing it when I could.

I started to teach Vladie some tricks, nothing fancy but she always liked to train and she even taught herself a few things- the little show-off. Back then, I was still fashion designing so I had fashion magazines around a lot. Vladie came up to me while I was reading one and started sniffing the magazine with real interest. I could not figure out what on earth she was smelling and she would not leave me alone. So I flipped the page and read some more, telling her to leave it. She would make eye contact with me then sniff the magazine again. Finally, it dawned on me that she was smelling the free perfume samples in the magazine. At first, I just laughed and patted her head and went back to reading until medium-sized paws landed on my arm. I thought, "Okay, you want to see it? Fine." So I showed her the page with the sample on it and she smelled it then she licked it, daintily. I was grossed out and said, "Vlad, don't lick it! Yuck!" But then I laughed and she left me alone. From that day on, Vladie would check out all the magazines, smelling for the perfume samples and she could tell which of the magazines were the fashion ones from the others. Oh… and if she liked a particular scent, she would sniff it a couple of times then lick it. If she did not care for that fragrance, she would back up a couple of feet and do a half sneeze, half cough and walk away. No kidding! I remember a couple of her favorites were Giorgio Armani's Sensi, Ralph Lauren's Blue, and Romance. (Yeah, she had expensive taste.) So I would tear out the free samples and lay them on the floor and watch Vladie choose her favorites. It was a cute game but later I would find out that it had been a good way to stimulate Vladie mentally; a mental game that helped her brain stay active and train her to use her nose.

Chapter Three

*I*t was not long after Vladie's graduation from Connie's puppy class that we decided to sign up for the next level training class at the same store. We got the other good dog trainer, Lindsey this time. Her approach to training was different from Connie's. Lindsey was a shorter woman with short blondish hair and a quieter personality. She was kind, softer-spoken and more timid but knowledgable and helpful.

Vladie had grown some and was more confident but she was headin' into her teen years- (oh boy---help!) So she was starting to act like she had not been trained at all. I feared we were facing some tough times ahead, so Lindsey's class proved to be more of a challenge for me. I was still nervous and a bit uptight about messing up and Vladie was starting to pull her own weight and damn, if she didn't. Even though she was not a purebred shepherd, (she wasn't as big or as tall), she did have power in those muscles. Many a time after class or at home, training, I would end up with sore hands and shoulders from her pulling.

I have to admit I was the one that was spoiled. Why, you ask? Well, when Vladie was very young, she was potty-trained without too many problems; she didn't chew up too many of my things nor did she do the nipping/mouthing for very long either. She had lulled me into a false sense of security, the little sneak. So when she got into Lindsey's training class, Vladie hit the terrible twos which caught me off-guard like deer in a car's headlights. But having said that, Vladie was actually very good in comparision to many other dogs I had seen or heard of.

Now, I cannot recall Vladie's classmates; I know there were two or three but I cannot remember them clearly. I think Vladie and I tried to keep focused on the lessons so playtime was no longer as important, but it should've been. The leash walk was still a problem for us. We muddled through for eight more weeks and…. Vladie STILL managed to christen the store's floor at almost every class. We did graduate but I knew that neither one of us was done with training.

Once the basic training class was done and she got her certificate and picture taken, I had heard of a local dog club so I investigated it. I got the information off of the internet and my parents and I went to a meeting. It was held at a retirement home that looked like a mini hotel and club members brought their dogs to it. We learned about classes that the club's trainers offered- agility being one, which caught my attention. So I asked my mom if we could sign up. I was not sure if she would go for it since the classes were held at the club president's home agility yard and that was a long driving distance for us. But she agreed- (thanks, mom!). So we applied to become members of the club and we had to be voted in by the existing members, which we were. So Vladie began to join my mom and I for the meetings. Vladie would follow me in and I put down a blanket for her by my chair and she would lay there, nervously. She was still timid but she would let people pet her and let other dogs come up to her but they worried her more than the people did.

Once we were official club members, we enrolled in the agility class and Vladie's new trainer, Grace was a short brunette and she was terrific! Vladie liked Grace, who was very informative, funny and encouraging. Grace nick-named Vlad as Vladie-girl and Vladie would come to it but only for Grace. Vladie had four classmates this time but the Australian shepherd, Amy was her favorite. They would roll around in the dirt- legs flying, tails thrashing and leashes tangling all the while Amy's pet parent and I would chuckle and try to keep order. Vladie learned to walk the plank, jump through the tire jump, go up and down the A-frame obstacle and walk over the high dog walk. But the teeter was the one she never felt good about. It took a lot of coaxing just to get her to put a paw on the teeter and then she would jump right off. I was afraid she would break a paw doing that. I would sometimes lose my temper, out of concern, and plus, I still worried about us failing the class, so I was self-conscious. I was the one with the issue, not Vladie, I admit it. But Vladie loved the class; she liked to run and jump and be outdoors so Grace's class, to her, was da-bomb! Oh and we did graduate, Vladie got her certificate and yes, I framed that one too. My mother even took a class picture of the group.

After that, money was getting tight so classes had to be put on hold for Vladie and I so we continued to work at home. I began to go to work on a portion of our yard and made a workout yard for Vladie. My father found a few cement blocks and some left-over plastic pipe so I made a simple jump out of that. Next, my father talked a worker at the dump into giving us an easel-like thing that we attached a used motorcycle tire to and so there was our tire jump. I bought a cheap set of weave poles and two more pole jumps but knew I wanted more equipment. I just could not afford to get it all at once. I also bought some metal stakes and some cheap field fence and put it up which proved to be a challenge to keep up in one piece. (The rabbits and the wind loved to chew it up or pull it loose.) But Vladie didn't care that the yard was not fancy; she just knew she had a play yard and she loved training time.

Because we are creatures of habit, as I'm always saying to my clients, our dogs "chain" our behaviors. (This means that they watch us, they figure out that one behavior leads to another certain behavior until we get their leash and put it on, for example). By then, they are usually quite excited and can be a challenge to get them to sit long enough to hook the leash to the collar. Vladie was slightly different regarding this. She would sit but it took treat motivation. Anyhow, she knew by the clothes I put on what was going to happen. She would follow me, just like the pipe-piper, to the bathroom and would watch me pull out my sweats from the shelf. She would start to get excited then. Her tongue would loll out of her mouth, her brown eyes would shine, those large shepherd ears always up like radar and her fan tail would start to cause a draft. I would dress and reach for my shoes and she would be bouncing around, like Tigger on his spring tail, then when I finally started down the hall, she would be running back and forth from the back door to me. It would take a lot of impulse control on her part to sit at the door and wait for me, to step out first then call her to follow. Nope, it did not work on the first try even after she learned it; she was just so excited. I held my ground though, letting her know that going out to train was a reward for waiting at the door.

Well when we finally made it out the door, she would go racing off the porch and out to search for wild rabbits and squirrels. Only when I called her and she saw I was going in another direction, did she follow me into the new agility yard. She happily sniffed it and checked it out then I took her to the equipment I had earlier set out and gave her the commands. She hopped over and through them like a pro, loving every minute. To keep things really interesting, I would then use the chuck-it toy (which was a godsend for me because I am no Yankee pitcher) and she would race after it. (The Chuck-it is a long handled ball thrower, in case you did not know that.) Most of the time, Vladie would bring the ball back, then after a few throws, I would switch to the Frisbee. When she had done that for a bit, then we would walk the fence line so her muscles could cool off. (Note- your dog should always warm up and cool off before and after doing any physical activity.) If I was still up to it then I would pull out the basketball to play soccer. Why not a soccer ball for soccer? Well, Vladie managed to puncture a soccer ball with her teeth when she would pick it up to steal it off the 'field'. This happened every couple of weeks which was getting costly so I got a basketball. A basketball has a tougher hide and they lasted a little longer. Notice I said…..alittle longer…Yep, Vladie still deflated one of those every year. But… as my friend, Matt would say those were…."Good times."

But once again, I digressed. After we would work out and I groomed Vladie, I would then take a shower. When we were both squeaky clean and worn out, I would sometimes sit on the floor and look out the open window, just enjoying the breeze. Vladie would join me but for a different reason. Her hawk eyes were always searching for the rabbits and squirrels that would scamper around in front of the window. The wild quail and ravens would gain her avid attention too. She would often stand the entire time just looking intently for the critters. I could only chuckle and shake my head as I either watched the sun go down or read a book. These were some of the best times. Just a relaxing, calming time for both of us.

Chapter Four

Vladie loved training. I usually wore out before she did, but like most dogs, she did have an Achilles' heel. The leash walk was always a challenge. Chasing ravens, wild rabbits and squirrels was more fun than walking politely, in her fuzzy, doggie mind. But her biggest issues were being in crowds and fear of water. (She would drink it but no way in Hades would she step in it). So you might be wondering how I dealt with these challenges. Well, to deal with Vladie's fear of crowds,....that was an on-going problem. I would take her out to doggie events that the humane societies would put on and though she was stressed, I tried to praise her for being good. I know I still made mistakes with her social skills training and I tried to rectify them. After some weeks, she was slowly improving.

I always continued to work on the leash walk, which in my training experience, is usually the hardest to teach and takes the longest to get a good handle on. Walking a dog can be a nightmare and I know you are all nodding when I say that. So I would continue to walk Vladie as often as I could and we would do our exercise routine too. I practiced what I preach. When Vladie would pull, I stopped and waited for her to come back or make some slack in the leash. Then we would be off again until five seconds later when she would do it again. Then I stopped yet again. I would do sudden turns to gain her attention and help her learn to watch my feet. It would take some time before we made it to our destination. (Talk about teaching us, humans, patience). The routine would go on like that until my shoulder hurt and my arm felt like it had been pulled out a few inches longer. We would end the lesson on a good note even if the training had not gone as well as it could have. Why? You want your dog to enjoy training and being with you so if you end a lesson all frustrated and take it out on your dog, your pup is not going to want to hang out around you. Let's face it- would you want to hang out with a friend who was in a bad mood a lot? You want to end a lesson on a happy note so that it is the last thing your dog remembers from the lesson.

Now back to Vladie's fear of water. I have no idea how or what caused it but from her puppy hood, she did not want any part of a bath or pools. Puddles were like sink holes to her- nope, no way, no how was she getting' wet. So, determined one summer to help her and make bath time more tolerable for both of us, I bought her a child's plastic wading pool. I put it out in the agility yard and hoped she would start to go to it during her workouts. I wanted her to put her paws in it because dogs have sweat glands in their paws and when submerged in cool water, it helps cool the dog off. But no matter how hot she got, Vladie still would not step in. She would sniff at the water, obviously thirsty, but she would go over to the small water bowl for a drink instead. One day, I moved the pool to another location, filled it with water then I put her on leash to lead her to it. She hesitantly followed and I treated and praised her for coming with me. Next, we would walk around it and she would sniff it so I would treat and praise her again. I tried to lure her into the pool but she would fight that. Not sure what else to try, I stepped into the pool, which she watched, alertly but would not follow. She would then psyche me out too- make it look as if she was going to follow me in. I would quickly give her a treat but then she would do a refusal- (an agility term), and back away. The little sneak. So we would start over again with the process. Eventually, I ended up sitting in the water, thinking Vladie would squeeze in beside me. (I was so delusional). I ended up with thirty pound dog climbing onto my lap, making sure not even a toenail touched the water! It took a few more tries, a few more days and A LOT of treats before she would finally step into the pool on her own. Even though it was only a paw at a time, she was learning to overcome her fear of water. I then moved the pool back into the agility yard and had to keep verbally encouraging her to use it but by the end, Vladie was walking in it, standing there under the wooden canopy and drinking the water at the same time. Now that's training, my friends! It takes persistence, patience, encouragement, rewards, and making good associations for your pup or adult dog.

Around this time, I began trying my hand at more tricks with Vladie. She first learned to extend her foreleg and drop her paw into my palm on command, which yes, is called the Shake. She then learned to sit up on her hinde legs but was always a little tipsy. (Quick note: most large breed dogs and some tiny dogs should not do this trick. It's too hard on their hips and joints). Vladie did not do the 'Sit up' too often for this very reason but she knew how to do it. She soon learned to bow, to hunt for a specific toy that I would hide and she knew one toy or one object from another. She was a quick learner for the shell game. Remember in the movies, a guy on a street corner sets up a table, has three cups or conch shells upside down and he hides a marble under it? Spectators watch as the man shuffles the shells around and they bet on who can guess accurately as to the location of the marble. Same game here but no bets…the currency is a tasty treat that's under the shell. Vladie picked the correct shell every time, using her nose which got her a handful of treats as reward. Learning the 'Roll over' was an unforeseen challenge to her. She knew the 'Down' command and did it reliably but she was not comfortable with the roll motion. It took her two days of very short practices for her to feel comfortable enough to roll over. When she got it, she never forgot and would do each roll with enthusiasm. Then Vladie would immediately pop up from the down position, smiling and waiting for the treat. Can't ever forget those treats!

After this, I began to try to get back to doing some hobbies for myself. I wanted to learn how to speak Italian. So I bought the language cds and a book from the bookstore and began listening. I learned a few words at a time and referenced to the book for the meanings. But this got me thinking. A trainer had given me advice once about dogs who had heard the same command in English so many times that they ignored the command after awhile. (This is why pet parents should not repeat commands too much while training.) Anyhow, I remembered that trainer had said to give the same command but in a foreign language and teach the dog to do the behavior to it. So guess what? Vladie began to learn Italian too. I wanted her to stay interested in training so I taught her the 'Sit', 'Here', 'Come',

'Miss' and 'Good' in italiano and she got them all within two days. That's my signorina!

Vladie learned how to pick up and carry a small bucket, a stuffed purse toy and even a fuzzy dog-shaped purse by the handle. I would tell her to take the doggie and she would pick it up by the purse strap and carry it around. Occasionally, she would flip it up in the air and let it drop. I am soooo glad that it had not been a real puppy. Eek. My mother got a kick out of the purse toy. It looked like one but it was assuredly a dog toy. Mom would say that Vladie looked like she was ready to hit the mall. I also taught Vladie some of these tricks with the clicker method and she did well with the clicker.

My friend, Matt took a liking to Vladie even though he did not see her very often. I sent him pictures over the cell phone of her and he would call and hear all about her latest accomplishments or silly antics. Then he began to ask me to put the phone down to her ear. Knowing Matt as long as I have, I knew he was up to something. I reluctantly did as he wanted. I could hear his voice but not the words clearly as he said something to Vladie. She leaned back, as if surprised, looked at the phone receiver and then... walked away, clearly unimpressed. I had to laugh and told him she had not been interested in the conversation. He chuckled. He tried again on another day and again, I put the phone receiver down to Vladie's ear and this time she licked the phone as Matt said hi to her! Yeah, that's what I said. Her big pink tongue came out and slid over the phone. No, I did NOT train her to do that and I laughed so hard, completely taken by surprise. From that time on, anytime Matt called and I lowered the phone to Vladie, she licked the phone as she heard his voice. Matt just loved that and of course, his response when I told him was, "That's hot." This just goes to show how you can reinforce any behavior with your dog visually or with sound, so make sure you really want that behavior to be encouraged, no matter how cute it is.

Vladie had a thing for phones. Let me clarify- she taught herself the phone trick with Matt that I just described so I bought her a cell phone toy for her. It was a real dog toy that looked like a pink cell phone and when it was squeezed, it would ring a few times. I taught her to pick up the phone when it rang. Cute, huh? But...she taught herself something else that wasn't so endearing. I am told that she did just what children do to their parents. (I don't know for sure, since I don't have kids). But every time I got on the phone, whether I answered or dialed it, Vladie would go to toy box, find every last one that had a squeaker in it and spend my ENTIRE conversation either squeaking each toy or dragging every item out so when I turned around, I would fall over the toys. How many times did my poor friends have to listen to endless squeaking in their ears and my complaining to Vladie to be quiet, I can't say. Then just as soon as I ended the conversation and hung up the phone, Vladie would look at me and lay down, all worn out. I can remember saying to her, "Why couldn't you do that a half hour ago?" Of course, she didn't reply. It was now her naptime. Ahhh, you just gotta laugh.

This was a bit of a creative time for me. I started writing poetry again and Vladie was sometimes the subject of a few of them. I also began seeing that Vladie naturally looked straight into any camera and posed. She seemed to like doing it so having been in the local art association for three years, I had a lot of artistic influences. I began to make a photo book of her. At first, it was just pictures of her doing regular activities but then I decided to make it more artistic, something memorable with flair. So I bought a lot of odds and ends from the craft store to design each page and make the pictures stand out. Each page was kind of themed in relation to the photo. I then began to pose Vladie in specific settings, and in her doggie outfits. I even created a backdrop out of display board and lots of fabrics. After a couple of short times of posing her, all I had to do was set up the backdrop and say, "Vladie, its photo time." she would follow me in and go sit in the display. She would stay in the poses and watched the camera flash. I guess you could say she was a photo hound or doggie diva. But still, she enjoyed.

Chapter Five

Soon, I realized I had to start earning my keep again, so I went out to look for a job. I found one at the petstore that I had been volunteering at, with the humane society. Once the job began, I am sorry to say, Vladie's socializing and education began to suffer a bit. I was working so much, as a cashier, that I could not get a lot of time off to take her places. (Vladie was around two or three years old). I could not go to the dog club meetings very often either so Vladie was not out making new doggie friends. (I also had to give up volunteering with the pet rescue too, due to my work schedule). The few times I did manage to take her somewhere, I saw how timid her behavior was reverting to, which concerned me. (As I now tell my clients, if you don't use it, you'll lose it). Dogs can learn many skills but if they are not continually reinforced and repeated, they will lose the skills. So I made that mistake with Vladie's education; I let it slip some but I did work on the lessons we had learned and the new tricks at home. Vladie's mind was always eager and willing and she liked training of any kind so I tried to do what I was capable of.

Later, Vladie had a new companion, Julius. He was an adult, domestic, long-haired cat. He had yellow/green eyes and was a gold/cream/white colored cat. I adopted him from the same rescue I had been volunteering with. (Since I had been working with that rescue for about four years at this point, they allowed me to adopt Julius even though I have allergies to cats. Julius was my miracle kitty but this is not his story, so that's a tale for another time). I was not sure how Julius and Vladie would get along but Vladie, once again, amazed me and so did Julius. Julius, in the beginning, tolerated Vladie but as the years progressed, they became friends....well, sort of. They had their own way of ...shall we say...communicating. Vladie would chase Julius around the room, he would hiss at her and roll over on his back. She would stand tall and frozen, staring down at him, just waiting and he stared back. Then like a flash, he would take a swipe at her with his paw and Vladie took the cue. Game on! She would go into the playbow and bark at him then stick her nose in his face. Sometimes, she would duck her head just in time and other times, she would be too slow for that little paw coming straight at her. I would hear, crack! as Julius's paw made contact with Vladie's dark snoot. She would shake her head for a second, (I imagined cartoon birdies were tweetin' around her head) then her tongue would loll out of her mouth, excited and she would charge him. Julius, seeing the error of his ways, would jump up and race for the nearest high spot which was usually his carpeted cat tree. He would hang out up there as Vladie would whimper and fuss for a few seconds, staring longingly up at him. I always thought, watching this scene, if Julius could have laughed, he would have been. Vladie would hang her head and walk away then happily bounce over to her toy basket and drag out half the toys until she found one to play 'bad

There's no way I can write this story without telling you about our holidays here. We had family traditions, probably like most of you but even Vladie, Baby and Julius had theirs. So basically here is a Christmas morning at our house. My mother would wake my father and I at dawn, practically, then we would take Vladie and Baby to their potty spot outside. Vladie would start looking for squirrels and rabbits, unless her bladder won the battle first. Baby would go in her pen, barking at the world while all of us froze from the cold air or the snow. Then once all of us got back inside, the heat having been turned on, Baby and Vladie would have breakfast. My mother would be laying out the hidden presents from her closet that she thought we did not know about and dad would be snacking on something and making himself a cup of coffee. I would feed Julius his breakfast, change his litter box and then get dressed. Mom would usually be calling down the hall by now to get moving so we could start opening the presents. Vladie, having munched her meal down, would be trotting back and forth through the house, getting excited. (After the first year, she learned fast what Christmas morning was). So I would put Julius in his cat stroller. Yes, he had his own chariot befitting a reincarnated roman emperor. Do I believe he was a reincarnated roman emperor? 'Course not but I think Julius thought he was. Anyway, he would go into his stroller and I would roll him out to the living room, put on the Christmas music on the cd player and when everybody was seated then I started handing out the presents. During Vladie's four years, she got the most presents; it varied by year but she had fun. On her second Christmas, Vladie tried to open everyone's presents but after a few 'Leave it' commands, she backed off but…she just watching the whole thing and probably thinking we all belonged in a padded room somewhere. But Baby got presents too- she wasn't as good at the opening part as her big sis though and Julius got goodies too but he preferred to partake of them when he was back in his house in my room.

Halloween was a big deal here. I loved it- my favorite day of the year so I usually decorated most of the house by myself which can take about a day. I even decorated Julius's house since it was his birthday, and Vladie, well, remember there's that vampire reference and gothic influences that she's named for so she enjoyed too. Some years, I had a big party and other years, it was a fancy small dinner for a few friends and us but either way, Vladie liked it. She would stroll around the house, after all the decorations were out and she would set off all the sensor-talking gravestones or the animated characters. At first, those scared her but she learned just to ignore them. Anyhow, Julius would come out and cautiously walk around the house. His eyes would be as big as saucers as he looked at all the enormous hanging skeletons, the lite-up pumpkins, the waving ghosts and the standing vampires amongst all the other décor. But you know, Julius parked himself inside the pumpkin patch set one year. Another time, he plopped himself down beside Vladie next to the witch's broom and cauldron. I swear, they both looked like they were part of the décor or a scene from a movie.

The only other holiday we, as a family, sometimes did something for was Easter. During Vladie's years with us, it was not a real big event here but one game I taught her and it's one I do recommend to my clients for this holiday, was the easter egg hunt. I bought a bag of the plastic easter eggs that open up and put training treats or pieces of hardboiled eggs in them then I hid them around the house. When ready, I gave Vladie the 'Hunt' cue and she had to find them and when she did, she got another treat. When all the eggs were found and put in a basket, I opened them and Vladie got to eat the treats. I know what you're thinking-it's just like a kid's easter egg hunt. That's the point but this version allows the dog to get in on the action and they love it. So next Easter, give this game a shot. Just remember, use your cue words like 'Go find' or 'Hunt', then say 'Bring it' and 'Drop it'. Finish the exercise with 'Okay' when the dog is allowed to take something. If you don't distinguish the dog's game from the children's, you dog won't understand and he will be stealing your child's candy eggs and that is NOT a good thing for his tummy or your carpets.

After about a year as a cashier, which is one of the hardest jobs anyone can ever do, I was starting not to enjoy life as much. Vladie and Julius were my stress-releasers, for the most part but I knew Vladie still needed more training, especially socializing. I was starting to feel guilty. I was tired all the time and was having a hard time motivating myself to get back to our routine. I knew she did not understand when I came home from an eight hour shift why I was irritable, run-down, just wanted to take a shower and go to bed. She would be scampering around and trying to kiss me. I would hug her and was glad to see her but I was stressed out. She did not understand why I did not run outside with her to play for hours. After a few minutes and watching my movements, (again, an example of chaining the behavior), she would realize I was not going to put on the exercise clothes and take her out to play. Moping, she would lay down on the floor, her head resting on her paws and look up at me, sadly. That look, ah yes, we have all seen it on our dog's faces at some point. It's that soulful, pitiful look that just begs us for our attention. We are all suckers for that look. We, pet parents, should be careful not to give in to it, no matter how hard it is. So the next time your dog puts his head on the dinner table just as you are about to lift that fork off the plate of a juicy steak meal and you feel those eyes on you- remember, your dog is training you!

On my days off from work, I did focus more time on Vladie. During the spring and summer months, we got out more. She loved her playtime. We had a routine. We would warm up, exercise, train and play in the yard then we would come back in the house and I would give her the cue for the grooming session. She would jump onto the grooming table and for about thirty minutes, I would brush her to remove all the weeds and check her for any injuries. (I think she could have been either a catcher for the local baseball team or one hell of a base stealer because she could catch any ball thrown and she loved to slide into a stop. Hey, are the Angels or Yankees hiring?) Anyhow, she would scrape her back legs up sometimes, on the dirt and rocks so after the brushing, I would wipe her down with pet bath cloths or doggie shampoo cloths and medicate any injuries.

As a sidebar for that subject there was only one time when Vladie really did herself harm. We were out in the yard and she was chasing the frisbee. The wind caught one particular throw and whipped the disk right into the yucca tree's trunk base. Vladie went barreling after it, ignoring my 'Leave it' command. It all happened so quick, though I was running to reach her but she had done it already. I grabbed her as she was backing away from the tree and noticed below her left eye, there was a blood spot. I felt my heart stop and wanted to cry. An inch up and her eye could have been lost. Playtime was over and I led her back into the house. If she could have had her way, we would have continued to play. (Dogs have the mental wiring in their brains to hide injuries as well as they can because if they were feral or surviving out in the wild, and were injured, they would be the first on a predator's hit list). Vladie was good at hiding injuries from me but I was a keen observer and would often catch a subtle misstep which indicated sore muscles, for example.

I digress a bit so back to the Frisbee incident. Vladie followed me into get groomed. I pulled out the cloths and began washing the eye area. She flinched a few times but did not seem to be in pain. It only looked like a small puncture in the skin and was not bleeding very much. So I began to disinfect it. I will spare you the gory details here but to wrap it up, my mom had to help me. I held Vladie still and mom used a tweezer to pull out a piece of tree bark that was no thicker than a sewing needle but was the length of the knuckle on my thumb to the end of my short fingernail. This scared both of us though, so I called the vet and got her in an hour later to make sure there was no other problem. She was put on antibiotics for a week or two and I kept it cleaned out. But from that time on, she had a little white line scare there and….she listened to me when I said 'Leave it' around any trees. Tough way to learn a lesson though.

When we were not treating any injury, our grooming sessions were relaxed. I would use paw moisturizer and massage her paw pads. If she needed a hair trim, I would do that and I wipe the dirt out of her ears with ear wipe cloths. The teeth was the last thing I would do and I taught her from puppy hood to tolerate a cheap electric toothbrush so I could take care of that. Then she got doggie mouth spray and doggie fragrance sprayed on her and lots of treats. If we had had a long workout, I would turn on the instrumental music, lay her down on the grooming mat and massage her muscles. If she was REALLY dirty, I would give her a bath in the tub. As you can see, hygiene and her health was very important to me. I read a book about dog grooming and how to make it fun for both owner and dog, by doing a doggie spa day. It changed how I thought about doggie bath time. Now, I tell my clients to spend time on their dogs' health and grooming. It helps detect problems before they get bad, gets the dog used to being handled and to the grooming procedure. It is worth the time, ladies and gents; believe me, as you will read why later on.

So my work schedule continued on that path for another year. During that time, my favorite manager saw how well I had been publicizing the dog training program there. I even earned the distinction of selling the most classes for the trainers. So my manager said one day, "Why don't you apply for the dog trainer program to be a trainer?" Honestly, the thought had never crossed my mind. I did not consider it at first, but it eventually got me thinking. So I started investigating the program. I had a good repore with two of the trainers on staff, so I asked them for advice. They told me about websites, authors to look up, books to read and said to start doing my homework. That was how I began my career change. For that entire year, I did research, bought training books and contacted Vladie's former trainers who kindly began mentoring me online.

I started keeping notes from dog training shows, bought training dvds and kept journals of my notes taken from all the books I had read. Management was now aware of my desire for a position change but after a year, I realized it was not going to happen, which depressed me further. I made good use of all the information I was getting and reading, with Vladie. She and I were trying to bump up our training sessions. I started to teach her to ring a hanging bell on the back door to let us know when she wanted to go outside. That was not easy and she never learned to do it reliably but she understood the concept. She was learning some more tricks, and we were still contending with the leash walk.

Growing more discontent with my cashier job, I began to put applications out to other stores. They were not what I really wanted either but I thought at least they would be different place; a change of scene. For a few months, nothing happened until one night, my mom agreed to go with me and Vladie to the other petstore in the area for their free training class. I thought it would be good for Vladie to get out and meet new dogs and go to a different place for a change. We went and had a nice time, met some new people but Vladie was very timid. The trainer commented on it but as the hour drew to a close, Vladie was calmer.

We went again for another free class a couple of weeks later and the other trainer, Danni was teaching it. She impressed us too. She had asked all of us about our dogs, what training they had had. I explained that I was hoping to become a trainer and was studying on my own to achieve the goal. As we were leaving, she told me that the first trainer I had met there, had left suddenly and that I should apply for the job online. I had already done so a few days before, thinking it was a long-shot. She gave some tips to help Vladie relax a bit, but Dannie said getting her out for socializing was the only remedy.

Chapter Six

I had resigned as president of the Art Association due to my job too and was missing the extracurricular activities. I wanted to do something with animal rescue again. I had met the manager of another local pet rescue when she came to the store. So I called her and left a message or two to see if I could volunteer. Tamara was very nice when she called back and I went to her home to fill out the forms and started assisting that day. She had a very nice place built for the dogs and puppies she was housing, awaiting adoption. She showed me how she wanted things done so I timidly began to work. She had stainless steel kennels in her garage for the young puppies and for the ones who had just been groomed for show. I was instructed to clean those out and disinfect the kennels. I swept out the area and fed the puppies in the big playpen on the floor. Then I proceded to follow Tamara outside to her brick-walled yard. There were chainlink pens of different sizes that had little dog houses and large water bowls and the ground was pebble stones. I used the pooper scooper and then rinsed out the water bowls to refill each. Each pen contained give to seven dogs of various mixed breeds. I tried to greet the pups so they could get used to meeting a new person. After all, gotta keep our four-legged friends always socializing. Some of them were very cautious and did not want to meet. Others were barking and on the defensive and some were glad to see someone and would jump up on me, trying to get attention. All the pups looked good, well-cared for and I was pleased to see that. Tamara then said to follow her to the largest area which was her patio where her own dogs, two great danes were. They seemed like nice dogs. She needed help bathing them so I assisted and both of us got quite wet in the process. When all the outside work was done, I went inside and helped bathe the young puppies with a young girl who was also volunteering. I did not like her way of bathing the pups, which was terrifying the poor things. (I knew from Vladie's phobia of water that her trouble could have been caused by rough handling during her first bath and I feared that these pups would suffer the same). But I did not attempt to instruct the girl.. Often times, advice calls on deaf ears and I was the new volunteer; this young teenager was not. So the puppy I was handling got better treatment though he was still not happy with the water in the bathtub. I used gentle handling, talked to him and did not drag him under the faucet but used my hand to cup the water and rinse him off. I began to towel him off when the girl took him from me, suddenly and walked out of the bathroom with both pups, whining. I watched, shaking my head, disgusted. I knew that some day some trainer or owner was going to have a water-fearing dog on their hands. Now I kick myself for not saying something at the time or at least kicking the girl on the way out. Ha ha. Alittle while later, my mother returned to pick me up and she came into the garage area to see the puppies. Tamara said she was always looking for

when they saw her. Compared to them, she was huge, very dark with the big, stand-up ears and probably looked a bit imposing. So I cued her to 'Leave it' and back off. She did, reluctantly. Every time I went in to check on them or clean them, she followed and for the first two days, the puppies were afraid of her but Vladie behaved herself. She would look at them then walk around the room, not caring or reacting to their freakouts. She would sometimes sniff the crate, making the pups squeal and huddle together, away from Vladie's big snoot sticking through the wire. At first, I thought she was purposely terrorizing them, not sure if she wanted to meet them or eat them. I would cue her away. There were times that she went into the room and I heard the pups. So I would have to go in and ask her what she was doing. She would look up at me with a look on her face that said, "What are doing keeping them in my crate?" I would send her out of the room.

When the pups came out of the crate to play on the shower curtain that I used as a floor mat, I kept Vladie out of the room but she could see through the baby gate at the doorway. She would whine a bit, wanting to come in and her whining would startle the puppies. They would eventually creep over to the gate and stick their noses through and Vladie would greet them.

After a couple of days, I let Vladie join them and hoped there would not be a problem. Vladie had not been socialized with puppies since she had been in her first training class so I was wary. I stayed calm and watched. The puppies were now more curious about Vladie but still careful. She would walk around the room, casually as they frolicked and peed on the newspaper and potty pads. I would rush to clean it up and put new ones down. Scarlet got brave and went up to Vladie and tried to stand up on her. Vladie did not hurt the pup but she gave a quick growl and jumped away from the puppy. I made the training sound Vladie knew that told her I was not pleased with that. Vladie backed off and Scarlet looked startled but then Nibbles approached Vladie and I cued my canine daughter to behave. As I watched, I soon realized that Vladie was not being mean to the pups, she was instructing them! She was telling them to behave just as I was telling her to. After a few minutes, I relaxed and sat back and watched the scene unfold. Vladie seemed to ease up a bit too as the puppies scampered around, grabbing the toys and tried to get Vladie to play. Vladie jumped around the room with the pups in tow and it seemed she now had a fan club. After that, I trusted Vladie with the puppies and they looked forward to seeing her. She would go in sometimes when they were in the crate, napping and check on them. I always knew when she did that because I would hear the pups from the other room, starting to rustle around when Vladie walked in. But I also knew when she had left the room because the pups would start whining for her.

We only had them a week or two. I think it was a fun learning experience for Vladie. She actually seemed depressed when I took them back to Tamara's rescue for their adoption day.

We later fostered a second litter for Tamara of four Chihuahua mixes- three boys and one girl. This bunch was a handful. Their personalities were clear from the first day and Tamara told us we could name them. My mother really liked that and Tamara laughed at mom's reaction when she told her. So we named them Zorro, Wilbur, Timber and Katie.

Zorro was the wildest of the bunch. He was a grey/tan color with white markings and his eyes were outlined with little black markings that almost looked like eyebrows. But it gave him a zorro-like mask appearance. He was the leader of the little pack. Timber was very similar in color to Zorro but had more charcoal markings on his snoot and was taller than the other three. He was sweet but could hold his own when he felt pushed around by the others. He was energetic and wanted attention. He would try to climb the wire pen to get out or to get someone to pick him up. Wilbur and Katie were the smaller of the four and often stayed together. Both were more skittish and were tan-colored with distinct, white markings that varied a bit. Wilbur was a roley-poley kind of fella with a sweet personality and more submissive. Katie was sweet but seemed more insecure than her brothers since she whined more often.

Vladie seemed to welcome this new bunch but they were leary of her, at first. But Vladie was now in the groove, having had practice with the first litter. She began training this rambunctious group from the start. The boys that I named, Timber and Zorro, were bold and bouncy. They began jumping on Vladie and she took them in hand, or rather…in paw. She was often growling at them, telling them to back off but she began to bring out her own toys from her toy box and offer them to the pups. Zorro and Katie would latch onto the big toy and Vladie would just gently hold onto it an they would all play tug. Vladie began another game too with the pups. She would race around the room with the puppies in tow and then she would spin around, plop down onto the floor and lower her head down. Katie and Wilbur, especially, would try and climb onto her back. She did not allow that but as long as they were nice and did not pull her fur, she would tolerate them trying. Vladie amazed me. I was proud of her and she seemed to have fun.

We had this little group for about three weeks until Tamara called and wanted them back for the next adoption day. So we packed them up in the carrier in the evening and Vladie was there, watching them go. She followed me to the kitchen and was going to go with us, I think but mom told her to stay. My mom was crying as the pups left. She had gotten attached to them but that's the issue with fostering. They are not yours to keep. I was fine with it though I had liked Timber the best but I had Vladie and did not want any more dogs. It would not have been fair to her to bring in another dog since my time was already so limited with her. As I went to the car, passed the puppy room's window, I saw Vladie staring out, watching us, intently as we drove away. We dropped the pups off to Tamara and I gave her the form I had written up, telling her what we had worked on with training, a bit about each dog's personality and any issues they were having. We came home and my mom informed me that Vladie had stayed in the puppy room, howling for about ten minutes straight, then ran from room to room to the back door, clearly upset. When I got home, she greeted me at the door, like usual and seemed happy to see me. I knew she noticed the pups were not with me and she checked out the yard when she went for her potty break. She came back in, sulking alittle. When I cleaned up the puppy room, took down the crate to sanitize it and picked up the shower mat, Vladie again searched the room for her four students. She then sat down and just watched me. I felt bad that she was depressed and decided not to foster again since it had been a teary experience for my mom, plus, I was worn out. I was still cashiering, trying to take care of myself and train Vladie. I was exhausted.

The day after the pups had left, Vladie was no longer looking for them and things went back to normal but this had been a learning experience for her too. She had proven to me that she could handle being around young dogs, successfully, unlike her feline brother, Julius and Baby, I might add).

I was still waiting to hear about any of my job applications and was growing concerned. Things at my current job was getting hairy due to the economy having trouble. Cutbacks were happening and I was growing increasingly worried and tired. I was often sick; kept getting colds and had to miss work more. I had to make a change and soon. One day, I got a break. I stopped into the other petstore and asked about my online application. They said to leave a resume, so I did. I saw Danni, the trainer again and she asked if I had heard anything. I said I had not. We left, went home and few hours later, I got a call from the store manager to come in for an interview. I was thrilled, got tongue-tied but was happy. A week later, I had the interview and a few hours after that, the manager called me and said "Tell your store goodbye". I did, that night, giving them a week's notice. A week later, I was at the new store, going into their dog training program.

Since I knew I was going to be busy learning the new job, doing the training, I did not have the time to foster puppies or do much volunteer work so I had to resign from Tamara's rescue. I continued to donate to them for awhile as money permitted. So feeling jazzed about my career change, Vladie and I were doing more studying together and I began working with her more. We still needed work on the leash walk but it was slowly improving. I wanted her to come to work with me, but Danni, who was now my training mentor, said I could not do that until I passed my Dog Training Instructor Exam and was actually training dogs. So that idea had to be put on hold for a short time but I knew it would help Vladie socialize better. It would also help her confidence level. Yes, dogs need to gain confidence, like us. So for all you doggie owners, get your dogs out and meet other dogs and strangers. Sitting in a big yard with four other dogs that they see every day, all day is NOT socializing. It's just…hang time which is boring and unchallenging to them. So do puppy playdates, take them shopping in dog-permitted stores. Do an outdoor sandbox for toy-hiding fun and interaction. Work out that boredom and stored-up energy! You will feel better, your dog will be happier and more tired. Remember, a tired dog is a good dog.

Chapter Seven

Five or six months had gone by, I had passed my Dog Training Instructor Exam and had started teaching classes. At first. I only had private classes but I was also doing the free classes, called seminars. I wanted to bring Vladie to work on seminar days but I was wary. How was she going to react? Was she going to mess the floor up as she had always done in the past? So I did not bring her for months but continued to take her to the public doggie events whenever I was able.

Later, when I felt comfortable, I began taking her to work with me and yeah, she did mess the floor up each time. Aargh! The first day she went with me, she was nervous, antsy and did not want to be there. She kept pulling on the leash to get out of the mesh ring we used for our students and out the electric doors. She would not do any of the behaviors she had been taught. She would not even try to do any tricks which she liked to do. She did not drink any water and she would not take any treats. She was scared and yes, this is typical doggie behavior if the dog is uncomfortable, stressed, scared or all of the above. Knowing this and not wanting her to be nervous, I thought about refraining from including her in my job. But, as I tell my clients, if you allow the dog to hide in their fears and never expose them to the source of fear, they will never get over it and learn how to be confident. So, I practiced what I preached. I tried to take her to work with me once a week and by the third week, she was calmer, enough to do a wave, a sit up and a bow. She was starting to relax a little quicker each trip and that was progress, which is the name of the game.

Danni began to offer the AKC Canine Good Citizen class and she had just earned the title of CGC Evaluator. This meant she could offer the test to customers to earn the CGC certificate from the American Kennel Club. I had never thought about Vladie earning that certificate until then. So after a few weeks, I went ahead and took Vladie for the test. Danni evaluated her. She had Vladie do a leash walk with me, a sit/stay, down/stay, walk amongst staff members who made lots of noise. Then Danni took Vladie's leash and told me to disappear for a few minutes to see how Vladie would behave or cope with my leaving her with a stranger. I went out to mom who was waiting in the car and counted the seconds, practically. When I went back to them, Danni was kneeling beside Vladie, who was sitting quietly but looking around anxiously, for me. I asked Danni how she did. She did well, I was told. So Vladie passed and she was now a Canine Good Citizen.

But that's not all she wrote. As we were about to leave, Danni was rubbing Vladie on the chest and being a veterinarian technician student, she was giving Vladie a quick exam. She looked up at me and asked when I had taken Vladie to the vet last, and did I have the shots updated? I was taken aback by the questions so I could not recall the exact dates of the last appointment but it had not been very long since our vet had last seen Vladie. She was up to date on her shots, that I knew and I told Danni so. She continued to rub Vladie's neck and chest. When she told me there was large bumps on her and they could be something serious, I was concerned. I felt for them myself and yeah, there were two bumps that felt like the size of golf or tennis balls on her chest. I was alittle ticked off that Danni would indicate or think that I had been negligent about Vladie's healthcare but I was concerned. I thanked her for giving us the CGC test and for her time and took Vladie out to the car. I felt a sinking feeling inside. What should have been a great moment was now somber and I was not pleased with my fellow trainer at the time for ruining it. But, yet, I knew that Danni was looking out for Vladie; that she was trying to help.

My mother was thrilled that Vladie had passed her test. She had wanted to come in and watch and take pictures but thought it might be too distracting to Vladie and I. It would have been, so I am glad she restrained herself this time. As I got Vladie into the car, on the backseat and buckled her in with her car leash, I told mom what Danni had said; that Vladie needed to see Dr. Barton. My mother did not want to hear that. I did not like saying it. Mom said that she was sure it was nothing. She, like me, remembered that Vladie had just been to the vet for a checkup a few weeks before and she was fine. We drove home, our moods dampened. Vladie crashed on her designer, paw print, doggie seat cover. She was exhausted and slept all the way home, a sign of the fact that she was still uncomfortable in the store but she had been a good girl.

I made the appointment to take her to our vet a few days later. Dr. Barton was really good and I trusted him.

He knew his stuff. I figured he was going to say it was a tumor, or a growth that would require surgery. I was already stressing over how, we or I, was going to pay for the surgery and treatment. We took her in and he examined her closely. Vladie was scared, as usual, but she did not pee on the doctor nor did she bite or growl at him. She never had, thank heaven and Dr. Barton was really good with her. He took her temperature, asked me some questions about her eating habits, bowel movements, irregular behavior, which I had not seen up to that point in time. Then he looked at my mom and I and said, "Its not good." My heart sunk but I knew it would not be. I was still expecting to hear the word, surgery. I braced myself as my mind still raced, trying to think of how I could pay for the operation. His next words stopped all thought. "I would say without x-rays but I am almost ninety-nine percent sure, that it is lymph node cancer." Everything stopped for me. I could not mentally grasp the words. I knew he could not be wrong but yet...he had to be. I suddenly thought, "This cannot be happening". My emotions were slowly creeping up on me. My mother, who was doing her best to keep a grip on her emotions too, said "Are you sure? Cancer. You're absolutely sure?" Dr. Barton answered, yes. I think he felt my mother did not trust him since she kept asking the question. I knew why she was asking. She was getting upset. She was shocked, first of all but also, because she, herself was recovering from her latest occurrence of cancer. It seemed almost too much for us both to take. I stared down at Vladie who seemed fine, looked good but was panting because she was stressing out. I started crying, quietly. Dr. Barton, who was being as sensitive and calm as he could, said that Vladie would not recover and she would get progressively sicker. The lymphnodes on her chest, the ones on the back of her legs were swollen and he expected the set of lymphnodes in her stomach to be enlarged too. He said he wanted to run a blood test on Vladie to be sure so he excused himself to get the equipment. Mom and I just cried. My mother got up from her chair, came to hug me which made me cry harder, though I did not want to. I ran my hand over Vladie's head and hugged her quick. When Dr. Barton returned, I was alittle calmer. He gave us the very limited and very expensive treatment options. One choice was for six weeks straight, we could bring Vladie into the office and they would give her doggie chemotherapy through an IV for a few hours a day. If she made it then she would get a couple of weeks off, so to speak, from the chemo but would have to return for the whole process to be done again.

Since it was chemotherapy that was very much the same as it is for us, humans, it was going to be very expensive and it would not give Vladie any quality of life. It would only extend her life a few months. I just could not cope. My mother was clearly upset; borderline of being angry and being sad. I told Dr. Barton I would let him know what we were going to do but I could not make that decision at that moment. He understood. We paid and left, still crying as mom and I got Vladie into the car. I lifted her onto the backseat and I put on her special car-buckle leash and she rested. I remember mom saying, "She doesn't act sick. She looks good, has been energetic and happy." I had to agree but as I thought about it, I started to remember that there had been a few times that Vladie had not been herself.. She had been sick there for about four or five days when she would not eat. At the time, I thought she had food poisioning. When she did try to eat, she threw it up so she stopped eating. She was tired, did not even want to get up and go outside unless I really motivated her. That had been about a month before. It could have been the first sign of the cancer creeping in but I cannot prove it and I did not recognize it as such then. Plus, at that time, I was still doing our grooming routine every other day and the swollen lymph nodes had not been apparent then. Dr. Barton had said too, that the illness is still a mystery. It can be passed on genetically or something in the environment can cause it. Aside from that, it can be dormant in the system then something sets it off and it starts to show signs rather quickly.

Mom called my father, who had stayed home and told him the news. He was stunned. Mom and I drove home and my father was waiting at the back porch steps as we parked the car. I let Vladie out to go potty and started to take her inside. My father patted me on the shoulder, said he was sorry and seemed to want offer me comfort. I did not want comfort. I could not respond. I was just too choked up. I took Vladie into the house, into the puppy room to groom her. She took her time following me but she came. I felt conflicted and upset as my jumbled thoughts kept distracting me. Vladie could no longer jump up onto the grooming table so I lifted all fourty pounds of her up onto it. She was tired and was panting a bit from the car trip but by doing our usual routine, it seemed to calm us both down.

I did some serious thinking for the next couple of days and tried to think where could I get the money for the treatments. I did not make enough salary to afford it and my savings was nearly gone. I wanted to help her, to save her; she was my little girl, after all but there was no money available. I did not own anything of value that I could sell. I could not get a bank loan either, since I don't own any property. Mom and dad would have helped but they had already begun to pay some of the Vladie's vet bills for me and were struggling to keep our household financially afloat. Beside that fact, Dr. Barton and two of his vet technicians all said, at different times, that the chemotherapy would not save Vladie; that it was going to cost at least a couple thousand dollars and it would only prolong the inevitable. Vladie would be exhausted, not herself either. I really felt conflicted. What should I do? That was what was so frustrating. What could I do? I kept asking myself that. I cried and lay awake at night, watching Vladie sleep in her plush, couch-like bed. It was a very hard decision but in the end. I had no choice. I had to choose not to pursue treatment. I felt like I was going insane. I felt guilty too. I cried more often and wanted to throw things every time I thought about it.

Vladie was weaker now but she wanted to exercise anyway, until she tried. My little trooper! She could have put the armed forces to shame with her determination. She really wanted to chase her basketball and do the agility but I had to make her settle for a walk instead. She would try to run but did not realize her balance was off or she did not know she was too weak until she landed on her face. She would start to stand while I was rushing to reach her and pick her up. The stunned look on her face really got to me. I didn't know dogs could show that expression but there was no doubt that she was stunned. I lifted her up which was easier since was losing weight and brushed her off. I checked her for injuries and tears would sting my eyes each time that I had to pick her up off the ground. I would do my best to keep her away from temptation after that. I hid the basketball and I told my parents not to kick any ball near her or play fetch with her anymore since Vladie was too weak. She and I also avoided the agility yard too.

Her appetite continued to waver. She was eating one of the best foods, in my opinion- Royal Canin German Shepherd kibble but she got where she did not want it so her diet changed. Her food list consisted of hot dogs, cheese, spaghetti, bananas, carrots, Natural Balance food rolls, Natural Balance and Wellness puppy canned food. I tried to keep her on better foods. Except for fruits and vegetables, she had never eaten human food before. But I was limited as to what she would eat and be able to keep down. My father would eyeball Vladie's meals with interest and envy, not that his diet lacked the good stuff. He would peer into the bowl and watch me mix the variety in and was ready to pull out the taco shells from the fridge. I would just shake my head and say, "It's not for you." He would argue that it just looked so tempting. Silly man.

Vladie would eat but her portion size also changed. She would only eat maybe a third or perhaps half of her normal portion. It was hard to watch and know there was not much else I could do about it. I even began to add baby food in and Pedialyte, after Renee suggested them.

I wanted to keep Vladie mentally challenged since her physical training had to be stopped. So no more agility, no more jumping or running, chasing balls or catching Frisbees. It hurt to know she could not do any of it anymore. I did try to walk her sometimes and I had to say she and I never enjoyed a loose leash heel as much as we did than in those days. I needed to keep training with her, to keep her happy. We did more mental games- the shell game was one, which I have mentioned earlier but not in detail. This is one I often recommend to my clients that they can cheaply make or they can buy it from that well-known dog whisperer's toy line, which is what I did originally. How do you play this game, you might be asking? Get three Styrofoam bowls or cups and poke tiny holes in them. Next, put them on a slick surface either a tile floor or short table and hide a treat or small toy under one of those 'shells'. Pick a smelly treat or the dog's favorite toy with a scent on it that he will recognize. You want to make it easy until the dog learns the game. Then shuffle the 'shells' around while the dog watches, give the cue word like 'Hunt', 'Seek', or 'Find it' and watch the dog locate the hidden item under the correct 'shell'. When the dog touches the correct shell, reward him with another treat from behind your back or from your treat bag. As the dog learns this game and gets into it, make the game alittle harder by using a less smelly treat or a different item under the shell. The idea behind this is so the dog has to really work his eyes and nose to find the item. Vladie always liked this game, she would knock over the shell with her nose or slap it with her paw and sometimes the thin, plastic shell would pop up and smack her in her cute face or land with a thump on the floor. Either way, it was always a comical scene.

Another game I taught her was what I called the veggie game. I bought plastic food items from the toy store and using the clicker method, I first taught her the name of some of the vegetable toys. Once she learned that, then I taught her to find the right vegetable out of a bunch and she caught onto that really quick. Within twenty minutes, she learned five different vegetables and most of the time, picked them out, correctly. If you don't think your dog can learn this, you have a surprise comin'. Just come see me and your dog and I will prove it, as a number of my clients have learned. My mother stopped by our room as I was teaching Vladie this and she was amazed. I remember her saying as she watched Vladie dash from vegetable toy to the other on cue, "Rin Tin Tin's got nothing on her."

Having done more studying on training and reading trick books, I began to pick out things to teach Vladie but I wanted to continue my mentorship with a local trainer. Vladie's agility instructor, Grace was always giving me advice, online which I appreciated, but I wanted to work with someone closer to my home, in person so I was referred to Christine. She did not live too far from my home, she was highly recommended and was a fellow dog club member of mine. So I called her. She was very kind, gave me information and said I could attend her class that was already running. She said I could bring Vladie but when I told her my concerns about the cancer, (and Christine had lost a dog to the same illness), she suggested maybe Vladie had better rest at home instead. I agreed and began attending her classes alone which were great and it gave me a better understanding of the clicker method. When I came home from each class, I was eager to work with Vladie on something Christine had taught that night. One trick was 'Say sorry' and Vladie did that one perfectly. She would follow the hand signal and just drop, her head landed on her paws and looked up at me so sadly. She knew how to work the cute factor. I was so proud of her! I also began to teach her some of the rally obedience stuff too. That was alittle more physical so I was careful as to what I worked on with her. The last thing I tried to teach her was to read the cue card but it proved to be a real challenge for both of us. I was unable to devote enough time to it and by then, Vladie had become more fragile so I chose to stick to the things she enjoyed and knew well. Vladie was still sharp as a tack, mentally and she continued to wow me. She loved to learn. My mother commented that Vladie just enjoyed it so much and wanted to please me. If that was true or not, I cannot say for sure but it does make me a bit emotional to think that it could have been. I just enjoyed every day with her.

Chapter Eight

$\mathcal{A}$round this time, I began thinking about giving up on Vladie's photo book. After all, it was meant to be an artistic project only but with her days coming to a close, I decided to add the nostalgic picture to it. So I started including the cute pictures. It was now a memory book not wholly the artistic endeavor it had started out to be. I spent the time trying to continue with the theme pages and I was happy with it. Some pages were like a story book illustration, others were collages of shepherd pictures. One page was a surreal page with all sorts of critters on it against a fairy-like background. Another page was decorated with pictures of her favorite game- soccer with her basketball so the theme was sports. Each page was unique. It did get harder to work on it though with the constant reminder of better and healthier days for her. But I wanted to finish it. Still, there was some teary pages at the end of the book.

It took me awhile to get up the strength to tell Renee and Matt the news about Vladie. Renee heard about it first since she and I talked to each other almost every day. She was very interested and concerned when I told her that Vladie had to go to see Dr. Barton. She would text me often, especially if it was a vet appointment day and she would ask me to call her with the latest update. Renee was genuinely concerned and even did some internet research for me, searching for a treatment or miracle medicine. (Thank you again, little sis, for all that you did for us). She asked me what I was going to do and was saddened by my answer of not doing the chemo but was supportive. She knew my reasons.

The night I told Matt, I was working on Vladie's photo book and he happened to call at that moment. At first, we just idly talked like usual but I knew I had to tell him. I did not want him to be the last to know and I knew he would be affected since he liked Vladie so much. I think he said something like, "What's new?" or " How are you doing?" as a conversation-starter and I could feel myself suddenly getting choked up. I had to tell him so I did as carefully as I could, which was not easy since I am no good at subtlety. I am blunt but I really tried to tell him gently. Matt went speechless, seemed stunned and then after a long pause he said, " I don't know what to say." I think he sincerely felt bad. He asked me what kind of cancer it was, how did I find it and what could or would the vet do for Vladie. I told him what I knew. He got out his laptop as we talked and he began to look it all up. His interest and concern surprised me and was touching. It helped me to know he cared so much. I told him how I was going to start cleaning out her stuff- the toys, clothes, bed, etc. I recall him saying in response, "She's not gone yet!" He said it was good that I was finishing her photo book but not to get rid of anything just yet. He was right but I think he had a vision of me suddenly filling large trash bags with her accessories and hauling them out the door at that moment. Yeah, when I get determined, I have a tendency to start tossing and stuff just goes flying but that is not what I meant to do in this case. I wanted to plan better and have some mementos of Vladie and if I did it before she left then I could be more objective; you know, keeping things that really represent her rather than hold onto every collar, leash, bowl, toy etc as a means of holding onto her. This was important to me because when my first dog dogs, Snuggles and Cuddles died, I did not keep any of their stuff because it hurt too much to have the reminders. So of course, at this time and at this age, I regret that. (I only have one picture of Snuggles which isn't of the best quality and a few pictures of Cuddles along with her dog tag). I did not want not repeat that mistake. When Vladie came along, I made the promise to her and myself, that I would put in the time and effort to make her happy. So when this sad turn of events happened, I made the decision to save a few things of Vladie's as keepsakes, finish the photo book, make a little monument to her out in the yard and also create a picture collage for my wall. Having been a published poet in my younger days, I then added another tribute to her- I wrote a poem about her, "Vladie's Reqriem" which is included at the end of this book. I needed to express something in writing too as a way of saying goodbye. I wrote most of it before she left me because, knowing me, I would be too upset after to ever get it written.

I started emailing a few other friends including Vladie's former trainers and everyone was shocked, saddened and supportive, even offering emotional help. I was amazed that my mentors and other fellow dog club members all had had dogs with lymph node cancer. (This illness was new to me. I had never heard of it but apparently it is a common illness). So people, have your dogs checked out by your vet regularly!

I was also typing a column on zootoo.com which is a great animal site, so check it out and had many friends to whom I had connected with there so I placed an announcement of Vladie's diagnosis on my blog. The response was very surprising and touching. People wrote in, expressing their regrets, kind comments, best wishes and their stories of losing their dog to the same or similar illness. Some of them made me cry but the kindness of strangers was very uplifting. I thank all those people again, for their support.

During the next few weeks, Vladie took time outs. We would play mentally-challenging games and I finished my mentorship with Christine during that time. Vladie and I would take our evening walks around the yard. She finally did an excellent heel, close both off-leash but all at a slow pace. She would head up the wooden porch steps as if she was out of breath or in too much pain to make it but I would give her the 'Okay' cue and she would do it. Some nights I wanted to continue to walk so after she got on the porch, I would give her the 'Stay' command so she could rest, get a drink of water and relax while the breeze would cool her off. Then I would continue to head down our long dirt drive to our gate and before I knew it, there beside me, not three feet away was my canine daughter doing her best to walk with me. That's that hard-headed german determination! It made me cry then and still makes my eyes tear up now, remembering how she would not give up.

As the weeks pressed on, I began to see Vladie was getting weaker. She did not seem to enjoy the simple things anymore. She laid in her bed often and seemed uncomfortable in her own skin. More foods became undesirable and she was losing weight, no matter what or how much I fed her. Her lean-muscled body was getting frail, her face was looking more like just skin and bone at that point.

I sat on the porch with her, frequently and tried to hold her in my lap, which was not an easy feat to accomplish, let me tell you. My mother would sometimes join us out there, each of us lost in our own thoughts. I found myself thinking about all the things I wished Vladie and I could have done but didn't. I also thought long and hard about what to do. Was it time? Was she really that bad off? Was I ready to let go? I weighed the pros and cons of keeping Vladie with me and saw that I could not be selfish anymore. It had been four months since her diagnosis. I knew what I painfully had to do.

The next night I picked a spot nearby in the rock garden I had designed and began to dig a spot. It took me three or four evenings and my father helped but I had to watch him with his health issues so he didn't overdue. By the end, I was in physical pain and had cried a lot from the emotions welling up more than from the pulled muscles, as the shovel slammed repeatedly into the thick soil. I eventually had to accept a friend's offer of help to finish the digging since I was unable to physically do it. Within ten minutes, he had finished it. The next morning, I made The Call and set up the appointment with Dr. Barton for Vladie's final visit. As always, his receptionist was very kind, sympathetic. I went into my parents' bedroom to talk to my mother, who was resting. I calmly discussed what I had decided, Vladie's symptoms, and why I had decided to do what I had. Mom had expected that conversation to happen so she was not surprised. She got a little teary-eyed as did I but supported my decision and said it was all up to me. When my father arrived home from work, he joined us and I told him also. He cried too but agreed with my decision. They then kindly asked if I was going to take Vladie to Dr. Barton or did I want them to do it for me? I felt torn, uncertain. I knew I should be the one to go, to be with her for those final moments but I did think I could stand it, having done it once several years before. After some contemplating, I opted to accept their offer to take her. Even to the last minute, I stressed over that choice. Was that the right thing to do? Was it cowardly of me? Yeah, probably. I felt guilty for having my parents do it since it was going to be hard on them too but I had not asked them to do it- they had volunteered. Still, I knew that Vladie would be anxious going in the car and she might wonder for a second where I was but dogs do not think that way. She would soon focus on other things. She would not be thinking of me by then. So I had to sleep... or not sleep with my decision.

I texted Matt and told him what I had chosen to do and I called Renee to tell her. She was very sweet and offered to come over that morning to go to the vet with me. I really appreciated that but knew it would be hard for her to get a ride over. Besides, I was not going to be in good shape and I did not want anyone to see me that way. I knew it was not going to be a good day.

That night, I stayed up as long as I could. I wanted as many of the last moments with my girl as I could get. She, on the other hand, was content to curl up in her soft-bed and doze off. She laid her head on the arm of the bed and stretched out which was her usual position, and slowly went to sleep. She looked so tired, which was not usual and I found myself studying each line on her face. My Vladie had lost that inner fire; the light that shined in her eyes when she was happy, rested and ready to run. She looked like a senior citizen without the gray, I might add. I got up and sat down next her, which awakened her. She lifted her head quick and peered up at me with a questioning look. I petted her head and told her, "It's okay, Vlad, go back to sleep". She lowered her head back down with a sigh. My eyes began to water, my throat felt thick and I had to turn away. I stood up and tried to distract myself by reading a book but I could not concentrate. All sorts of things kept running through my head. I still doubted my decisions. Should I cancel the appointment? Maybe she was okay and would be okay if I just gave her some more time. But I kept looking at her and could see the misery she was feeling. I started thinking about the places I never took her to, the agility training I had wanted her to continue with, the other events we were being cheated out of. I had regrets, obviously, but I did try to focus on the positive. I remembered all the achievements she had accomplished. I thought of the places I had taken her to etc. It was not a big comfort at the time. I cried myself to sleep.

Chapter Nine

The next morning, I woke up in a daze; not sure what day it was until I saw Vladie trying to get out of her bed. My heart sank. This was it. There was still time to change my mind, I kept saying to myself. Was I really ready to let her go? Maybe she would feel better, if I just gave her more time. I watched her struggle to her feet, her unstable legs quivered a bit. Her little face really did look miserable. It was a telling expression; one of extreme effort and pain. I felt sick. No, she was not happy anymore and she was trying so hard. I felt my throat tighten again. I had to let her go, for her sake.

I took her outside to her potty area and let her do her thing. Then we came back into the kitchen and I made her some breakfast though I doubted if she was going to eat it. She proved me right. She just sniffed it and took a few bites but that was all. I tried to keep my inner energy normal, tried to keep to our routine. I did not want to feel any anxiety because I knew Vladie would feel it. My mother and father were subdued as they prepared their breakfast, fed Baby hers and did their morning routine. they did not say much to me as we got ready. Of course, that's a contradiction in terms. You can never be ready for something like that, no matter what you tell yourself. Plus, nothing anyone says to you at this kind of moment is any consolation, even though they mean it to be. You cannot be consoled, at least I could not. I did not want to discuss it anyway. I could not put the words to the thoughts I was having or the emotions that were welling up inside me like a volcano. Though I do believe in the calm and assertive method and even teach it to my clients, that went out the window this particular morning. I felt like I was on the edge of a cliff with the rational world behind me and the insane one of painter, Hieronymus Bosch leering before me.

It was an early appointment at the vet so I did not have much time. Vladie seemed not to notice anything was up so I must have been controlling my inner turmoil to a point. She was so tired and I put her leash, slowly walked her to the back door and we did our usual training of wait at the door and her following me out. I knew my parents were about to follow us so I walked Vladie around the yard a minute or two. She sniffed the ground, smelled the air, probably searching for her favorite nemesis- the wild squirrels. My parents came out the door and were heading off the porch so I led Vladie to the truck. I opened the door, feeling my stomach knot up. I wanted a miracle at that moment. It did not come as I lifted her up so she would injure herself trying to get up on the seat in the truck. (It was too high for her to jump and she was too weak). I waited there with her for a few moments while my mother climbed into the back seat beside Vladie. The look on Vladie's face as I petted her head made me want to cry. she knew then something was not right. Her expression seemed to say, "What's happening here? Aren't you coming too?" I closed the door as I told her I loved her and to be a good girl. My mother and I exchanged a sad but knowing look. I hurried away as my father got behind the wheel and started the engine. I nearly ran over to the steps and up the porch. The tears were filling my eyes and I could not see. Baby barked at me as I entered the house and followed me down the hall to my room. I flopped down on the floor in front of the window and watched the white Explorer make it's way to the gate with it's three occupants and go out onto the road. The thought of "Vladie is not coming back" seemed to hit my brain like a hot fire place poker and I grabbed the nearest item to me, impulsively. The item, I cannot even remember what it was, threw itself against the wall as if by some unseen force. The agonizing yell that accompanied this motion seemed to also come from someone or something else. When the item ricocheted off the wall and landed on the floor, I realized that I had thrown it. It was me yelling out my grief, that tight felling in my chest was also because of the sobs. I could not stop, wanted to stop, wished for something to happened to help me stop the crying. All I could think was, "This is it. Vladie and I will never get to take more agility classes. She'll never get to go to the beach for the first time. I won't be able to take her to work with me again. There will be so many things we won't ever be able to do now." My sobbing continued on for what seemed to be an eternity.

It was not an eternity before my parents returned home. Both were very somber and looked a bit teary-eyed but seemed okay. (I later learned from Dr. Barton that my poor parents had cried themselves through a whole box of tissues in his office). My father opened up the back hatch of the truck and he and I lifted out The Box. It was heavy and contained a bag, wrapped with a blanket. This was my girl coming home. I felt wrung out, emotionally and tried to focus on the task ahead. The grave spot was dug out and ready. I had laid out the shovels the night before and now it was time. My emotions were trying to get the best of me a gain. I fought them as I lifted the heavy bag out of the box. My father had said to wait, that he would help me but I ignored him. I could not for fear of collapsing in front of my parents and becoming useless. I lowered the bag into the hole while my mom watched. My father returned from the garage as I began shoveling the dirt into the hole. I did not want to say anything over the grave site. My throat was constricted and no words would come. I could not even think straight. My father joined me moving the dirt. I felt sick as I continued to shovel. When we were finished, my father took the tools back to the garage, my mom and I went into the house. The rest of the day I felt like I was in a somber, gray fog, mentally. I did not want to do anything and ended up watching tv to escape from the nightmare I now found myself in.

But later that day, I got onto the computer and emailed Vladie's memorial poem that I had written, to my friends, Vladie's trainers, family and to the internet friends from zootoo and myspace. This was my funeral announcement to them since I knew I would not be able to speak the words to them over the phone. Vladie was truly gone. Her bed sat there, empty. Her toys in her toybox still in their spot. I kept expecting her to come walking in with a toy in her mouth, prancing around, her ears up and her eyes shining with happy anticipation of a game. But she never came. I did not hear the light footsteps nor the squeaking of the toy from the other room or from down the hall. No, there was no sound, other than from the tv and Baby who keeping coming into my room and looking around, clearly confused. She knew something was not right. Everyone was home except her big, dark-colored companion. Baby walked around all the room, then back into the hall, just looking around as if strolling through the house but her eyes revealed her confusion. She even went over to Julius's house to check him out. She would later settle down next to my mother's chair for short periods but would bounce up at the slightest sound. I think she kept expecting Vladie to suddenly appear or come bounding in from the hallway and charging into the living room like she usually did. But no, this time, Vladie never came and I had no way of explaining that her big sister would never return.

Chapter Ten

*I*t took me a few days before I could get myself back onto the computer, wondering if anyone would acknowledge Vladie's passing. I told myself that she and I were really unknowns. My loss of Vladie, except for a few people, would go unrecognized but...the response I received was one that I never expected. Not only did friends and family like Renee and Matt, call or text me but complete strangers on zootoo wrote in too! I was very touched and to this day, thank all those people for their consideration and kind words. I printed out all of the emails and put them into Vladie's photo book. To prove this, I am including some of those comments here.

"...what we need to realize is that Vladie was sent for a reason and while it's hard for us to accept, it may be that reason has been accomplished and it's time for her to go home. (Yes, I do believe we will see our pets again!) I know this does nothing to ease the pain at this time."

"My heart goes out to you about Vladie. I have lost a wonderful cat to cancer-several years ago and I believe he's waiting for me at the rainbow bridge. There are many people here who can give you suggestions if you ask for them, listen to your advice if they need it and share in your joy and sorrows involving your pets. Our admiration for the philosophies of the Dog Whisperer and helping others solve their problems when necessary is what brings us to this list. Our fellowship with one another and our common experiences keep us here."

"I am utterly filled with grief over the news about Vladie's cancer. What a terrible thing...bless both of your hearts! I'll be saying prayers for both of you."

"G, let me know about Vladie. I wanted to let you know my prayers and thoughts are with you."

"It's the moments that take our breath away and Vladie sure continues to do that. May the comfort of others be a consolation to you and yours as mom told me the very sad, heartbreaking news about Vladie."

"Sorry to hear about Vladie. I'll keep her in my prayers."

"I am sitting here at the computer crying for all of you. My heart and prayers go out to all of you. This is so hard, words cannot express the aching in your hearts...we are all proud of M. and Vladie, what a cutie-pie."

"Oh I am so sorry...I know there's nothing I can say that is going to make you feel any better or make the pain any less. But I am sorry this is happening. I'll definitely keep you all in my thoughts and prayers."

"I am so sorry to hear about your loss and I know how hard it is. Love ya."

"May all the wonderful memories you've shared with Vladie help you through this sad time."

"He is your friend, your partner, your defender, your dog. You are his life, his leader. He will be yours, faithful and true, to the last beat of his heart. You owe it to him to be trustworthy of such devotion".-unknown. "No more suffering for Vladie. Good job, M. You are a wonderful mom. My heart goes out to you. Remember, Vladie will be waiting at the rainbow bridge."

"What a beautiful poem!…so sorry…love you."

"I was so sorry to hear about your loss…my heart goes out to you."

"I am so so sorry for your loss. I know it's hard. Huggz."

"MK, I'm so sorry to read that Vladie lost her battle. She was a very brave girl. You were very brave too. My heart goes out to you."

"What a wonderful tribute to your 'daughter'. I'm so sorry for your loss."

"Vladie could not have had a more wonderful life or a more caring mom. You are truly a dog's best friend. I know that you did all you could for your special Vladie and that she loved you above all else in return. I noticed the Vladie paws and picture plaque while I was visiting and thought about what a special partnership you shared. I know that Vladie is once again healthy and is practicing her agility routines as she watches over you each day from now on. I am thinking of you."

"Beautiful, heartfelt poem for Vladie. May the comfort of others be a consolation for you and your family at this time of loss. "Its better to have loved and lost than to never had loved at all. There's more room in a broken heart." Love and prayers."

"I'm so sorry to hear about Vladie. You have my deepest sympathy. It's always hard losing a loved one."

"I want you to know I'm crying as I read this. I am so sorry for your loss. I know those words never seem to say how we really feel, but every cloud has a silver lining.

Sometimes it's hard to see that when your heart is filled with sadness. I know how much you loved her, now you can share your love with another doggy in need. I hope you are doing ok…"

Dr. Barton and his staff sent a bereavement card which said, "Our loved ones may leave this place, but will always remain in our hearts. How precious the time, how beautiful the memories. We wish to extend our most sincere sympathies."…."Your sweet baby will always remember you."

Okay, readers, do you need a tissue yet? Believe me, after reading these for the first time, I was overwhelmed. Now that I read them again to type them here, I get choked up. Goes to show that animal lovers, do stick together when the tough times roll in. I thank those people who too the time to let me know their thoughts about my canine daughter. There are no words to describe the feeling of knowing so many people cared about Vladie and I. I did not even realize how many lives Vladie touched and some of them, she had never even met in person but her little antics, successes and stories I put on the computer allowed people to know her. I guess I know Vladie is not truly dead- she is here, in the memories, the stories, in this book and in the photographs and artwork. It's her monument to her short life.

As a way of coping with this, I heard of a pet bereavement class given by a humane society out of town. Not sure if it would help me or not, I was skeptical but when I mentioned it to my mother, She said it was a good idea. So I took the Saturday off from work and we drove down there in the early morning. It was a small class, given by two psychologists. They spoke for two hours on ways to deal with the grief of losing a pet and how to let go of the pain and guilt. One lady who also there, expressed both emotions since her little dog slipped out of an open door and was attacked by a coyote who was hiding in her yard. Another person was there because her beloved fish had died. The psychologists were calm, understanding and showed a slide show with music that wrung your heart. They explained that creating a memory piece like a keepsake box, a picture gallery, writing something as a tribute were healthy ways of dealing with the emotions tied to losing a pet. My mother told my father as we left that I had already done all that and both of them seemed proud of me. But the seminar was still very worth while and I was glad we had gone.

Some people say that there are spirits all around us. Sure, the shows on tv about ghosts make you think that and maybe there are. I am not going to judge that one but unlike one famous author who wrote that his golden retriever had come back to him in a form of a butterfly to say goodbye, I don't believe Vladie ever returned to me. I never saw anything that would lead me to believe she had performed a doggie visitation. Would it please me if she had? I am not sure. (Not sure having a doggie ghost following me around is a good thing). On the other hand, to quote Lydia from Tim Burton's movie, "Beetlejuice", she says, "The live ignore the strange and unusual." It is possible that I never saw the sign IF Vladie had sent one. But I will admit that every once in a while, I forget and start to call her name until it dawns on me, even a year later at the time of this writing, that she is gone. Once I did think I could have possibly seen her. Out of the corner of my eye, I thought I saw a flash of black and a fan tail walk past but I dismissed it. I don't indulge in the supernatural way of thinking.

I trust in the fact that she is in doggie heaven and since her feline brother, Julius joined her six months later because of the same illness, I envision him slapping Vladie in the snoot and Vladie hauling butt after his fuzzy tail until he jumps up on a fluffy cloud, dangling his paws just out her reach. I can see him practically laughing at her. Remember, my boy just LOVED teasing his big sister and Vladie....well she never got tired of that game. That is my remembrance of them both. This is what I choose to remember; my furry kids together and maybe even meeting their unknown siblings- Snuggles, Cuddle and their hamster buddy, Pepsi. I just close my eyes and imagine a beautiful forest scene with a waterfall and lots of critters running around. Yeah people, just like a fairy tale except here, the biscuits and training treats fall from the trees endlessly, the water bowls overflow with crystal blue water and the food bowls are always full with the best goodies. Yeah, that's doggie paradise. That is where I envision Vladie to be.

If I had to do all this again, knowing that she would be taken so soon, do you think I would do it? Damn right, I would. Vladie was a canine angel on earth. If I could say something to her in dogish, it would be "Play hard, and rest well, my Vladie, girl."

THE END

"VLADIE'S REQRIEM"

By
Maryann Keck

Once you were so small,
No bigger than a ball.
Sweet, cute and energetic too
From the rescue, I adopted you.

We laid side by side,
You learned to seek and hide.
Toys, treats, and games galore,
You always wanted more.

To classes we went one, two, three-
Learning how a good citizen to be.
Obedience, agility and later passing CGC,
I was so very proud of thee.

You loved your training, tricks and all,
You could never have enough of your ball.
You ran like the wind- free and fast,
A streak of black and tan flying past.

Artist's model you were, writer too.
You brought cheer to those you knew.
Perfume samples you liked to smell.
You learned Italian words quite well.

Licking the phone when Matt would call,
Dragging your toys down the hall.
You liked red, purple, silver and black,
For anything good, you did not lack.

You struggled on as best you could,
No more chasing Julius as you would
Keep smiling that doggie smile,
While lying on the floor that was tile.

When the darkness came on so quick
And the clock of life ceased to tick,
I held you close on the floor
Wishing for fun, games and time, more.

You rested you head against me slow
Your eyelids slowly drifted low.
I held you close and rubbed your ears.
I said goodbye, my eyes filled with tears.

VLADIE

(Jan. 2005-Aug. 2009)